THE FERTILE ROCK

SEASONS IN THE BURREN

THE FERTILE ROCK

SEASONS IN THE BURREN

CARSTEN KRIEGER

The Collins Press

Published in 2006 by
The Collins Press
West Link Park
Doughcloyne
Wilton
Cork

Text and images © Carsten Krieger

This book is not intended as an aid to navigation.
The author and publisher disclaim any responsibility for errors regarding light character.

British Library Cataloguing in Publication Data.

Krieger, Carsten
The Fertile Rock: Seasons in the Burren
1. Natural history – Ireland – Burren – Pictorial works
2. Burren (Ireland) – Pictorial works
I. Title
914.1'9300222

ISBN–10: 1905172028
ISBN–13: 978-1905172023

Design and typesetting: designmatters

Fonts: Sabon; Bell Gothic.

Printed in Ireland by Colour Books

Poulnabrone portal tomb (above)
and Crab Island at Doolin (opposite).

CONTENTS

Dedicated to Samson, who died too young to see the wonders of our world.
You changed my life. I will always carry you in my heart ...

and ...

in remembrance of John MacNamara, a true man of the Burren.

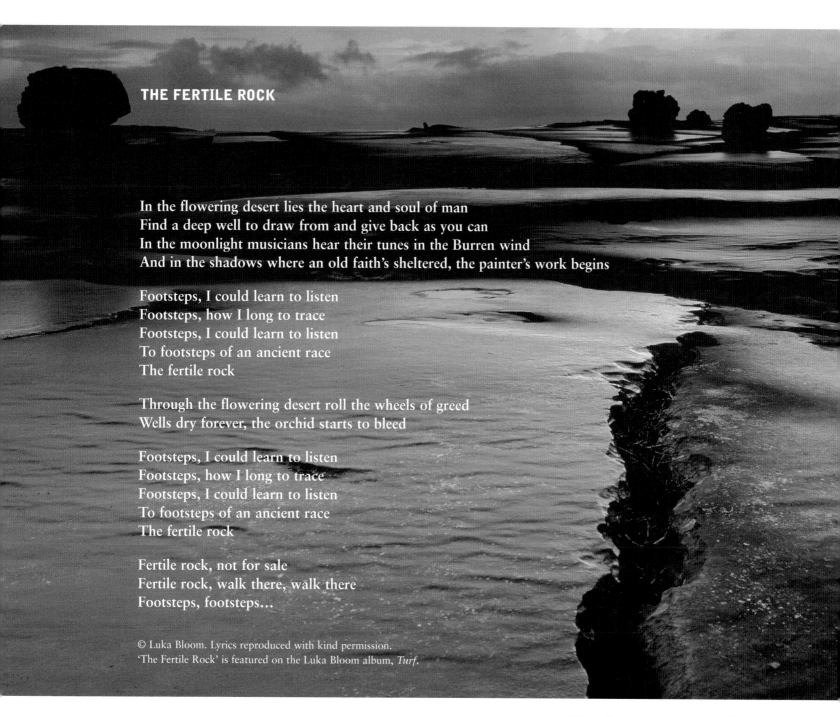

THE FERTILE ROCK

In the flowering desert lies the heart and soul of man
Find a deep well to draw from and give back as you can
In the moonlight musicians hear their tunes in the Burren wind
And in the shadows where an old faith's sheltered, the painter's work begins

Footsteps, I could learn to listen
Footsteps, how I long to trace
Footsteps, I could learn to listen
To footsteps of an ancient race
The fertile rock

Through the flowering desert roll the wheels of greed
Wells dry forever, the orchid starts to bleed

Footsteps, I could learn to listen
Footsteps, how I long to trace
Footsteps, I could learn to listen
To footsteps of an ancient race
The fertile rock

Fertile rock, not for sale
Fertile rock, walk there, walk there
Footsteps, footsteps...

Wintry limestone pavement at Ballyryan.

PREFACE

THE YEAR 2005 is still young as I process the final images for this project. The rain is striking at my window, the Atlantic roars, and somewhere in the far distance are the mountains of the Burren.

These last days have probably been the most magical I have ever experienced in the Burren. Snow is a rare event here, and that it happened at Christmas made it more special still. When I arrived at Mullagh More towards noon on Christmas Day I was welcomed by a blizzard, and wasn't able to see as much as a metre ahead. Lough Gealáin and Mullagh More were invisible – hidden by the clouds and driving snow. All I could see were dancing snowflakes, and all I could hear was the howling of the wind. I wasn't prepared for the scene that awaited me when the clouds cleared: a winter wonderland. The limestone pavement was covered in several inches of white, while Mullagh More and Knockanes wore snowy hats. It was pure magic.

There are many beautiful landscapes on our planet, but only a few like the Burren – a place that grips your heart and soul. Once the bottom of a tropical sea, and later covered by several hundred feet of glacial ice, it's not so long since it was covered by a huge pine forest and was home to brown bears (*Ursus arctos*).

I have been working on this project for more than two years, spending an average of three days each week in the Burren. Those regular visits to one of earth's most incredible landscapes became a central part of my life, and it's hard now not to be able to walk on limestone at least once a week.

I will keep in my memory those special moments that left me stunned and full of awe: my first sunrise at Mullagh More – a beauty beyond description; the stoat that managed to grab a chocolate bar from my bag; my first visit to the Oughtmama churches, where I felt closer to history than ever before; the day I found the Irish saxifrage (*Saxifraga rosacea*), a plant so rare that it grows only in a few isolated places in the Burren; or my first eye-to-eye encounter with a group of feral goats (*Capra hircus*).

Needless to say, it wasn't always easy. I began exploring the Burren years before I actually started work on this book; the most beautiful and magical places are far off the beaten track, and it takes time and patience to discover them. Coping with the famous Irish weather is a story many photographers can tell. Waiting is another one; waiting for the perfect light, waiting for the wind to die down – so as to capture a sharp image of a flower swaying in the breeze – or waiting for the creatures of the Burren to come out into the open.

Now I must finish *The Fertile Rock*, and those many images that still only exist in my imagination will have to wait to be taken some other day. I could probably spend the rest of my life taking pictures of this limestone landscape and its inhabitants yet still not feel my work is done or that I have taken my last picture of the Burren.

At the time of writing there are hopes and rumours that the Burren will be designated a world heritage site, so that it will gain the recognition and protection it deserves. It's my fervent hope that this book will contribute to the attainment of that goal, and make people – locals and visitors alike – more aware of the importance and beauty of the Burren.

Limestone cliffs at Ballyryan (above). Gorse (Ulex europaeus) near Lough Rask (opposite above).

ACKNOWLEDGEMENTS

There are many people without whose help this project would not have been possible. First and foremost I have to thank the late John MacNamara of Fanore. John was the first to support me in my plans, and was an incredible source of information and stories. Sadly, he passed away in 2004, but I am sure he is still watching over the Burren.

Many thanks to Luka Bloom for permission to reproduce his lyrics for 'The Fertile Rock', and for his beautiful music, which inspires me over and over again.

I would like to thank Maureen Comber and Anthony Edwards of Clare County Library for their continuous support, Emma Glanville of Dúchas for her help, and the staff of Aillwee Caves for taking me on a private tour so as to shoot some images for the book. A very special thanks to my editor, Dominic Carroll, for improving my 'German English'.

A big thank you goes out to the people of the Burren for enjoyable chats, countless cups of tea and for rescuing me whenever my car was stuck in some ditch.

And last but not least I wish to thank my wife Ina for finding the flowers I couldn't find, for viewing without complaint the endless stream of images I brought home, and most of all for being there. I love you.

Limestone pavement below Mullagh More.

CHAPTER ONE

A LIMESTONE WILDERNESS

The fertile rock lives up to its reputation; thrift (Armeria maritima), one of the most common coastal flowers, grows on tiny patches of soil on the limestone.

THIS WORLD is dominated by man, and we have left our mark everywhere. In only a few places on our planet does a sense of ancient wilderness survive; places that are not yet deprived of their natural spirit and magic, places that exist in their own time and remain immune to our destructive urges. Surprisingly, the Burren is such a place. Although inhabited by man since the earliest times, this solitary place appears unharmed by invaders. A peace and tranquillity prevails here.

The Burren is located on the west coast of Ireland. In olden days, when Ireland was divided into baronies, the northern half of County Clare formed the barony of the Burren. The region that is nowadays called the Burren doesn't exactly match the ancient borders; what we call the Burren today is slightly bigger than the old barony, and covers the northern half of County Clare and parts of south-east County Galway.

The borders of this limestone wilderness are not always visible. To the west and north, the Atlantic Ocean appears to form a natural border. Yet even this is deceptive, since the Aran Islands – a few miles off the coast – geologically and in terms of their flora belong to the Burren. Once connected to the mainland, the islands of Inisheer, Inishmaan and Inishmore are now an outpost of the Burren in the waters of the Atlantic. The southern and eastern boundaries of the Burren are even less obvious. A line drawn between the villages of Doolin, Lisdoonvarna, Kilfenora, Killnaboy and Corrofin roughly delineates the border to the south. To the east, the mountains of Mullagh More and Turloughmore and the adjoining freshwater wetlands form the border.

The name given to this area – Burren – is an anglicisation of the Irish word *boireann*, meaning 'big rock' or 'rocky district'. The area is one of the finest European examples of glaciated karst – a limestone landscape with underground drainage. The fact that limestone dissolves in water accounts for the strange appearance of the Burren landscape, and even more for the invisible network of caves and subterranean passageways. Underground rivers,

constantly replenished by rainwater, have taken their course through these caves and passages over the millennia.

There are many entrances to this Burren underworld but only one cave is safe to enter and open to the public. Aillwee Cave was discovered by a local farmer, Jack McCann, in 1944, and is probably one of the oldest and largest of the Burren caves. It leads into the very heart of Aillwee Mountain, with passageways of over 18 metres (60 feet) in height and 9 metres (30 feet) in width. During extensive surveys in the 1970s, bones and hibernation places of the brown bear were discovered; this animal is long extinct in Ireland. Aillwee Cave also features two underground cascades, and the biggest stalagmites and stalactites found in the Burren to date.

It is impossible not to be fascinated with the Burren. The bare limestone grows into terrace-like hills and stretches in a flat pavement up to the horizon. Erratics (huge limestone boulders) rest on clints (massive limestone blocks); these blocks are separated by grikes (cracks in the limestone that can reach several metres in depth) and dotted with dolines (rounded hollows that have been washed out by rain). In between these limestone mountains, green valleys appear almost as an oasis of life in the grey, stony desert. But there is life in abundance all over the Burren. Even on top of the barest mountain, some kind of life manages to survive on a patch of soil hidden in the cracks and hollows of the limestone. This life is what makes the Burren so unique and accounts for its attraction to botanists from all over the world. It is not that the Burren is a refuge for endangered plants, although some species growing here are indeed rare; rather, it is the combination of plant assemblies and communities. The mixture of species in the Burren is not found anywhere else in the world; plants that usually grow as far apart as the Arctic and the Mediterranean are here found flourishing side by side. Flowers such as mountain avens (*Dryas octopetala*) – which usually grow in the Arctic tundra – can be found together with Mediterranean species like the pyramidal orchid (*Anacamptis pyramidalis*). Other

(Opposite left above and below) Reminders of the Burren's distant past are abundant, especially on the western coast; these fossils are several million years old. (Opposite right above) The skeleton of a brown bear found in Aillwee Cave is thought to be more than 1,000 years old. (Opposite right below) The 'Praying Hands' are one of the most impressive stalactites/stalagmites in Aillwee Cave; these formations are made of pure crystalline forms of the mineral calcite, the main component of limestone. The oldest examples, found deep inside the cave, date to around 350,000 years ago.

Lakes such as Lough Gealáin are characteristic of the eastern Burren (left). Limestone is the dominant feature of the Burren, appearing as polished-limestone pavement (opposite below left) or as razor-sharp gravel fields (opposite below right).

plants are found growing in what for them are highly unusual and strange environments. For instance, the wood anemone (*Anemone nemorosa*) – a classic woodland plant – is thriving on the open limestone of Abbey Hill, and alpine species such as the spring gentian (*Gentiana verna*) – usually located high in the mountains – are abundant at sea level all along the Burren coast.

Although the Burren is most famous for its plant life, it hosts a rich fauna that is often overlooked. In recent years the Burren has developed a reputation for its remarkable community of butterflies and moths. At least 30 species of butterflies and more than 200 species of moth have been recorded, including the Burren's own Burren green moth (*Calamia tridens*). Most species can be found from April to October – with a peak in the summer months – though single individuals of peacock (*Inachis io*) and small tortoiseshell (*Aglais urticae*) can be found all year if the winter is mild.

Beside butterflies and moths, probably the most famous animal of the Burren is the pine marten (*Martes martes*). Almost extinct in Britain and on the European mainland, the Burren is one of the last strongholds of this beautiful carnivore. Other interesting mammals living in the Burren are the Irish stoat (*Mustela erminea hibernicus*) and Irish hare (*Lepus timidus hibernicus*). Both are Irish subspecies of their European relatives but differ in appearance. The stoat is smaller than the common stoat, and looks more like a weasel (*Mustela nivalis*). The Irish hare is related to the mountain hare of Scotland – an animal whose brown summer coat becomes pure-white fur in winter – but the Irish subspecies, having adapted to the mild Irish winter, has dispensed with winter camouflage; only a few animals still show a hint of white on their hind legs in winter.

Bats are widespread in the Burren; surveys have found seven species living in north Clare, including the rare lesser horseshoe bat (*Rhinolophus ferrumequinum*).

The Burren is a haven for birds. Only a few species are permanently resident, but there are a considerable number of summer and winter visitors. Tits, thrushes and finches are abundant all year round. Summer visitors include the willow warbler (*Phylloscopus trochilus*), whitethroat (*Sylvia communis*), cuckoo (*Cuculus canorus*) and the rare nightjar (*Caprimulgus europaeus*), all of which return to the Burren to breed. In winter, several species of duck, goose and wader reside in the wetlands of the eastern Burren and along the coast. The Burren's birds of prey include the peregrine (*Falco peregrinus*), hen harrier (*Circus cyaneus*) and the scarce merlin (*Falco columbarius*).

The Burren gives the impression of a uniform limestone habitat, but freshwater wetlands, shrub lands, grasslands, woodlands and various coastal habitats also abound. The most extensive habitats are the limestone and grasslands, which can be subdivided into lowland, intermediate and upland habitats. These three habitats are very similar: limestone – in the form of a flat pavement fragmented by crevices, and covered by an irregular jumble of loose rocks or fields of gravel – alternates with grassy patches and stretches of hazel shrub (*Corylus avellana*). The difference between the lowland, intermediate and upland limestone habitats lies in the floral life; the lowland and intermediate habitats host the richest plant communities of the Burren. Salt-resistant coastal plants, such as sea pink/thrift and sea campion (*Silene maritima*), proliferate close to the water. Further back and slightly above sea level flourish the spring gentian, mountain avens, bloody cranesbill (*Geranium sanguineum*) and many other famous Burren species. At about 200 metres, the profuse plant diversity of the lowland and intermediate type gradually reduces, giving way to the less-species-rich upland communities. These are of a heathland type – where peaty soil has formed on top of the limestone – or consist of naked limestone summits. Heathland, which consists mainly of ling/common heather (*Calluna vulgaris*)

and bell heather (*Erica cinerea*), can also be found in the lowland and intermediate limestone and grassland habitats.

The freshwater wetlands of the Burren are restricted to the east of the region. The only consistent surface water in the western half is the Caher River, which extends for about 4 kilometres before reaching the Atlantic at the Fanore dunes. The east-Burren wetlands consist of a system of lakes, turloughs (seasonal lakes that cover huge areas during winter and can reach depths of up to 10 metres), fens and cut-away fen, and extends for some 15 kilometres along the south-eastern boundary of the Burren. These wetlands are especially important for wildfowl – such as wild swans, wigeon (*Anas penelope*) and teal (*Anas crecca*) – which spend the winter in the area.

The Burren coastline is dominated by rocky shores. Only the dunes at Fanore and Bishop's Quarter, together with the salt marshes around Ballyvaghan, effect a change in the uniformity of the Burren's limestone coast. The Fanore dunes and the adjoining dune grassland on the landward side form a special part of the Burren. The rich yellow of the beach and the green of the dunes are in stark contrast to the overwhelming grey of the surrounding limestone. In summer and autumn, several species of orchids, such as the pyramidal orchid, the bee orchid (*Ophrys apifera*) and the rare autumn lady's tresses (*Spiranthes spiralis*), can be found here in abundance alongside many other flowering plants.

The salt marsh at the Rine Peninsula near Ballyvaghan is probably the most important coastal habitat of the Burren. Countless birds – among them brent geese (*Branta bernicla*),

shelduck (*Tadorna tadorna*), lapwing (*Vanellus vanellus*) and curlew (*Numenius arquata*) – spend the winter here, feeding in the nutrient-rich waters of north Clare.

The existence of these unique habitats – home to an array of fauna and flora – is attributable to the location of the Burren. Here, on the west coast of Ireland, the Atlantic Ocean provides a mild, humid climate all year round. But that was not always the case. The story of the Burren begins some 300 million years ago, during the Carboniferous period, when Ireland formed part of a tropical ocean's seabed somewhere on the equator. The inhabitants of this ocean were primarily shells and corals, which drew calcium carbonate – the main ingredient of limestone – from the water so as to build up their shells and bones. Following their deaths, these animals sank to the seabed, and over time their shells and bones were broken up, forming shell-and-coral sand and mud. For thousands of years, layer after layer of this material built up and gradually hardened into limestone. The shifting of continents and oceans over a huge expanse of time delivered Ireland to its current position on our planet, and today the fossils of those ancient animals, enclosed in the limestone, can be found everywhere in the Burren.

The limestone of the Burren had once been covered by younger rocks, such as shale and sandstone. Then, around 66 million years ago, the climate cooled rapidly, and a cycle of glacial advance and retreat began. These glaciers were the force that formed the landscape of the Burren. The protective caps of shale and sandstone were worn away, exposing the limestone; only at Slieve Elva and Poulacapple have outcrops of Namurian shale remained. Once the protective caps were removed, rain and melt water from the glaciers could easily percolate into the soluble limestone. Fissures became cracks, cracks became tunnels, and tunnels enlarged into caves. This process continues today, with every shower of rain washing away a piece of the Burren; in time, the Burren will be gone, washed back into the ocean from whence it came.

The last glacial retreat occurred around 10,000 years ago, at the commencement of the current warm period in which we live. Here begins the history of the famous Burren flora. The melting glaciers left a tundra-like flora consisting of Arctic and alpine plants. During millennia of continuous warming, plants from the Mediterranean spread northwards, joining the Arctic and alpine plants of the post-glacial Burren. Today, these species grow side by side in what for them are unusual conditions; the Arctic and alpine species have adapted well to a warmer climate, and the Mediterranean plants cope with the often cool and wet weather. But the future of this unique combination of plants is uncertain. Global warming and climate change, together with human interference, will seriously impact on the Burren in ways that are as yet unknown.

The fauna of the Burren has also changed greatly over the millennia, and continues to do so. Wolf (*Canis lupus*), boar (*Sus scrofa*), crane (*Grus grus*), eagle and the giant deer (*Megaloceros*) were once resident in the Burren and became extinct due to the loss of habitat and excessive hunting by man. A number of local place-names recall the presence of these creatures: Knockaunvickteera, near Lisdoonvarna, means 'the little hill of the wolf'; Keelhilla, which lies beneath the Eagle's Rock at Slieve Carran, means 'the wood of the eagle'.

The impact of humans on the Burren dates back at least 5,000 years. Prior to the arrival of man, the limestone was covered by a rich mineral soil that supported extensive pine forests up to the mountain summits. When the hunters and gatherers of the Neolithic period settled and became farmers, they changed the nature of the Burren forever. Woodland clearance was followed by extensive farming of cattle, sheep and goats, and was complemented by cereal cultivation. Thousands of years of overgrazing, combined with a deterioration of the climate in the late Bronze Age around 3,000 years ago, resulted in a substantial loss of soil, especially in the uplands of the Burren. The appearance of the Burren as we know it today is more than the product of nature and time – it is also the work of man.

Today, cattle-and-sheep farming is an important element in the conservation of the Burren. Animals that can be kept outside all year round keep fast-growing grasses down and make it possible for slower-growing plants to flower and to survive. An equally important role is played by the descendants of the early farm animals; feral goats living wild in the Burren – mainly on the higher slopes – prevent hazel and other shrubs from spreading and taking over the Burren.

Signs of human settlement are apparent all over the Burren: portal tombs and stone forts from a distant past, stone walls and 'green roads' built some centuries ago, the ruins of cottages only a few decades old. Despite this, the Burren appears almost unspoilt. Most buildings blend with the landscape, and some have become an

The heart of the Burren is a mixture of barren limestone summits and fertile valleys; a summer meadow in bloom is one of the glorious Burren moments (above right). Ancient buildings – such as ringforts and portal tombs – are often located beside modern dwellings (above left).

integral part of it. Though under European legislation the Burren is designated a protected landscape, most of the land is privately-owned farmland, and only a small part of the Burren is protected as a national park. Under the management of Dúchas, the Irish Wildlife Service, the Burren National Park incorporates ten per cent of the entire Burren area, and is located in the south and east of the Burren. The heart of the National Park is the mountain of Mullagh More. Beside its spectacular appearance, Mullagh More and the surrounding land is one of the most species-rich areas of the Burren. Orchids in particular seem to like it here; the rare fly orchid (*Ophrys insectifera*), lesser butterfly orchid (*Platanthera bifolia*) and autumn lady's tresses grow beside more abundant species, such as the heath spotted orchid (*Dactylorhiza maculata*), flecked marsh orchid (*Dactylorhiza cruenta*) and the Burren's own O'Kelly's spotted orchid (*Dactylorhiza fuchsii okellyi*). On the upper slopes of the mountain, helleborine (*Epipactis helleborine*) and dark-red helleborine (*Epipactis atrorubens*) can be found.

Two nature reserves have been established to protect small but unique places. Caher Valley Nature Reserve, the Burren stronghold of the pine marten and a sanctuary for birds, encompasses the only river of the Burren to run entirely above ground, through a small valley covered with hazel, blackthorn (*Prunus spinosa*), guelder rose (*Viburnum opulus*) and other shrubs and trees. Caher Valley is also a treasure trove for flowers: grass of Parnassus (*Parnassia palustris*), tutsan (*Hypericum androsaemum*), lords and ladies (*Arum maculatum*), water mint (*Mentha aquatica*) and several species of orchids are found in

abundance here. In summer, the shrubs form a dark-green barrier that blocks out almost all sunlight. In the twilight, dampness rises from the ground and the only sound is the murmur of the nearby river. It's a magical place.

Keelhilla Nature Reserve is located at the foot of Slieve Carran. At first sight, the scenery appears typical of the Burren: the limestone pavement stretches up to the foot of the mountain, and an ancient dry-stone wall runs parallel to it. In winter, cattle graze the scarce vegetation. Closer investigation reveals one of the densest accumulations of flowers in the Burren; in only a few places are there so many species in such abundance. Spring gentian, mountain avens, burnet rose (*Rosa pimpinellifolia*), goldenrod (*Solidago virgaurea*) and many others have colonised the patches of soil and found sustenance in the cracks of the limestone. A footpath leads to the foot of the mountain and into an enchanted forest. The tiny oratory of St Colman MacDuagh and its holy well is encircled by hazel wood and probably some of the oldest shrubs of the Burren.

No matter where you go in the Burren, every step you take reveals another magic place, and beyond every turn there is more beauty to be seen.

CHAPTER TWO

SPRING

Mullagh More – situated near the eastern border of the Burren – is one of the most impressive landmarks of the area.

A S FEBRUARY draws to a close, and while winter provides some final chilly and stormy days, spring is already waiting in the wings. The days are getting longer and brighter, and the first spring flowers signal the end of the dark season.

In early March, lesser celandine (*Ranunculus ficaria*), wood anemone and dog violet (*Viola riviniana*) are the first to appear, followed by marsh marigold (*Caltha palustris*) and primrose (*Primula vulgaris*) at the end of the month. From April onwards, the famous flower display of the Burren gets in full swing. Cowslip (*Primula veris*), lady's smock (*Cardamine pratensis*), hoary rockrose (*Helianthemum canum*) and the early purple orchid (*Orchis mascula*) – the first flowering orchid of the season – burst into bloom. The flower everybody wants to see, the pride of the Burren, is the spring gentian. They first appear in late April, and in May the deep blue of the spring gentian is almost ubiquitous in the Burren. Often found along with the spring gentian is the second orchid of the season, the difficult-to-spot dense-flowered orchid (*Neotinea maculata*), which produces flowers around mid-May. This combination of plants goes a long way to accounting for the appeal of the Burren flora.

Another special sight in early spring is the blackthorn; the still-leafless bushes appear pure white when laden with flowers. Out on the limestone pavement, blackthorns growing out of the crevices – where they are pruned by the wind and chewed by the goats down to rock level – nevertheless produce flowers. One of the few seasonal ferns also starts to thrive again in May. The widespread bracken (*Pteridium aquilinum*) is an unmistakable sight, growing up to a metre in height and often forming forest-like thickets. By the end of May, the Burren is in full bloom. Thrift, sea campion, Irish saxifrage, butterwort (*Pinguicula vulgaris*) and many others paint the grey limestone from seashore to mountaintop with every imaginable colour.

As the flowers revive, the butterflies and moths emerge from hibernation. The peacock and small tortoiseshell are the first to be seen, followed by the common blue (*Polymmatus icarus*), red admiral (*Vanessa atalanta*) and wall brown (*Lasiommata megera*), to name some of the most common. Moths are mostly active at night, and are often overlooked as they rest – camouflaged – on stone or wood during the day. One of the biggest and most beautiful moths, and relatively widespread in the eastern Burren, is the day-active emperor moth (*Saturnia pavonia*). The most famous species, however, is the Burren green moth; discovered in 1949. It is unknown elsewhere in Europe.

It is not only butterflies and moths that are attracted by the flowers; as soon as the first flowers are out, honeybees and several

The strange, sculpted appearance of the limestone is the product of retreating glaciers at the end of the Ice Age and several thousand years of rain.

species of bumblebee set about their business. Another sign of the long-awaited spring is the return in April of sand martins (*Riparia riparia*) and swallows (*Hirundo rustica*), the departure of the Burren's winter visitors for their breeding grounds in the Arctic, and – finally – the unmistakable call of the cuckoo.

April is a busy month for the Irish hare. It is mating time, and groups of females and contesting males – jack-hares – can be easily observed in open country; so distracted are they by their activities that one can get quite close to watch their very entertaining behaviour. A female hare can give birth to several litters over the spring and summer months, each consisting of three to five leverets that are born with a coat of fur and are soon fully mobile.

The rabbit (*Oryctolagus cuniculus*), badger (*Meles meles*), fox (*Vulpes vulpes*) and pine marten have already delivered their offspring by this time. Their young have been born blind and helpless in underground burrows, and another four to six weeks go by before the new arrivals leave the nest and see daylight for the first time. As the wild animals of the Burren produce their young, so too do the domestic animals. Lambs looking like cuddly toys, and long-legged, clumsy calves and foals are a common sight at this time of the year on the Burren pastures.

With the first warm spring days, the villages of the Burren also seem to awake from hibernation. Houses are given a fresh coat of paint, streets and roadsides receive a major clean up, and the first benches appear outside pubs and coffee shops. This is one of the busiest times for the farming community of the Burren, and a sixteen-hour working day during the spring and summer months is not unusual for a Burren farmer.

Beside the odd shower, spring is a dry season. The turloughs have usually dried out by May, leaving behind the remains of algae that become crisp in the sun and damp meadows where grasses accompanied by the yellow flowers of silverweed (*Potentilla anserina*) and the strange, tiny and inconspicuous adder's tongue (*Ophioglossum vulgatum*) – a relative of the fern – begin to thrive.

To sit on the slopes of Abbey Hill in the northern Burren early in the morning, to look out at the blue waters of Galway Bay, to feel the gentle breeze coming in from the Atlantic, while all the while being warmed by the sun, is one of those unforgettable Burren experiences.

Down in the south-eastern Burren, the mountain of Mullagh More is glowing in the evening sun. Lough Gealáin has given back a considerable amount of land, where grasses now grow almost to hip height. On the limestone pavement east of the lake, a colourful flower garden promises the coming of summer.

The abundant spring gentian – known as 'the pride of the Burren' – flowers from April to June.

The hazel is one of the most common shrubs in the Burren; male catkins (far right) and tiny red female flowers (right) can appear as early as January.

Carron Turlough, one of the largest seasonal lakes in the Burren, is usually completely dry by March. The sun further dries up the mud until it cracks and leaves a crazy paving appearance.

The lakes at Turlough have dried out, enabling hawthorn (Crategus monogyna) to burst into bloom (above). The Irish hare is still very common in the Burren upland areas (right).

*Mating gets underway for the great tit (*Parus major*), as it does for all the birds of the Burren. In many areas, the lack of trees challenges the birds to find alternative breeding sites (left). Abbey Hill in the northern Burren (below); a gentle breeze, blue skies, green fields and the grey of the limestone provide the ingredients for a perfect spring day.*

The primrose – ubiquitous, abundant and glorious – is a typical spring flower, showing its first flowers around March.

Leamaneh Castle, probably the most impressive building
in the Burren, consists of a fifteenth-century tower house
and a manor house built in the seventeenth century.

The burnet rose, though found elsewhere in Ireland, is a plant closely associated with the Burren; it begins to blossom in May and can stay in bloom until August (above left and right).

The Irish saxifrage – rare in Ireland but one of the Burren specialities – is restricted to a few localities between Doolin and Black Head; it flowers in May and June. Rather inconspicuous when not in bloom (left) it is a real eye catcher when flowering.

The dense-flowered orchid is another Burren speciality (above); less abundant than the early purple orchid and much smaller, it can be very difficult to find. The early purple orchid is the first of the Burren orchids to bloom (right); its flowers appear around April, and the plant can often be found together with spring gentian and the primrose.

The road around Black Head, where the slopes of Gleninagh Mountain drop into Galway Bay, is the most frequented tourist route in the Burren; crammed with cars and buses during the summer months, early spring offers the last opportunity for a peaceful glimpse.

The lighthouse at Black Head – the only lighthouse in the Burren – looks out over Galway Bay towards Connemara.

The Martello tower of Aughinish (above) was built in the late eighteenth century by the British to defend against a French invasion. The peninsulas of Finavarra (left) and Aughinish – stretching like two fingers into Galway Bay – are among the most beautiful places of the Burren.

The fresh green of spring in the fields of Bishopsquarter is welcomed by animal and man alike. In the distance are the grey caps of Slievenagapple and Moneen Mountain (above). The offspring of domestic animals appears in early spring; lambs are an especially common sight (left).

Opposite: Domestic animals play an important role in conservation; their grazing keeps down fast-growing grasses and herbs, thus ensuring the survival of the more-delicate flora.

The holy well at MacDuagh's hermitage (above) is hidden inside a hazel wood; a small oratory and other features are located nearby. Established around the seventh century, it became an important pilgrimage site in the nineteenth century, and remains so. In spring, ferns cover the ground of the ancient hazel wood (left).

In a remote valley below Turlough Hill are the three churches of Oughtmama. The monastery is thought to have been founded in about the eleventh century, and only declined in importance after the rise of nearby Corcomroe Abbey several hundred years later.

Fishing forms part of the economy of many coastal Burren villages. It is not always possible to go out during the winter months, and some boats fall victim to the severe storms.

The arrival of calmer weather in spring allows fishermen to once again venture out to sea. After some careful maintenance (above: 'old pier' in Ballyvaghan) the boats are ready to serve again for another season (left: 'new pier' in Ballyvaghan).

Spring at its best. Red valerian (Centranthus ruber) blossoms on grey limestone pavement. Hedgerows of white-flowering hawthorn divide green fields (above). A 'green road' ascends from Caher Valley along the slopes of Slieve Elva – one of many such roads in the Burren, some of which are thought to date back several thousand years to the very first settlers (left).

The feral goat is not a wild animal in the true sense; the herds that roam the Burren are the offspring of domesticated animals that escaped or were set free a long time ago.

The church at Killnaboy is one of the most interesting in the Burren. The west gable features a double-armed cross (right). Reliquaries that contained a fragment of the True Cross had been marked with a double-armed cross. So it is possible that such a fragment brought back by medieval crusaders has been kept at Killnaboy. Over the south entrance can be seen a sheela-na-gig (above right). Sheela-na-gigs are stone carvings of grotesque, naked, female figures striking a provocative pose, found in medieval churches and castles. Their origin and meaning is still widely discussed.

From late April, the spring flowers bloom. The sea campion (above left) grows all along the coast. The rare pyramidal bugle (Ajuga pyramidalis) (above) can be found at Ballyryan. The marsh marigold (opposite left) and the water avens (Geum rivale) (opposite right) are common in wet or damp places.

Typical plants of the open limestone are the blue grass (Sesleria albicans) (left), cat's foot (Antennaria dioica) (above) and the mountain avens (opposite right). The bracken (opposite left) is the most common fern in the Burren, despite its preference for lime-free soil.

In early spring, wild garlic (Allium triquetrum) forms a white carpet in the hazel woods of the Burren. On calm days, the smell of garlic in the air can be breathtaking.

Some typical woodland plants, such as the wood anemone (above) thrive on the open limestone hidden inside crevices. The barren strawberry (Potentilla sterilis) (left) flowers earlier than the wild strawberry (Fragaria vesca) (above left); unlike its relative, it produces hard, tasteless fruits.

The view from Abbey Hill across Ballyvaghan Bay to Cappanawalla and Gleninagh Mountain captures the peace and tranquillity of a spring morning.

If any shrub can be said to encapsulate the meaning of spring, it is the blackthorn. Its flowers appear before its foliage and, from March, the pure-white blossoms clustered along the black branches are one of the most beautiful sights in the Burren.

A common shrub in the Burren is the hawthorn; unlike the blackthorn, its leaves appear prior to flowering.

Showers can refill the turloughs, though usually for a short time; lower rainfall of the coming summer will cause them to dry out.

CHAPTER THREE

SUMMER

In a field near Kinvarra stands an old windmill, built probably in late medieval times before the development of the water wheel.

SUMMER in the Burren is a celebration. The days are long. The sun rises at four in the morning and does not set until eleven at night. There are sizzling days with deep blue skies, when the hot air shimmers over the limestone. There are days when a fog-like cloud covers everything, producing a persistent drizzle that leaves you soaked within minutes. And there are days when warm sunshine alternates with sudden heavy showers and thunderstorms.

The limestone looks like a colourful carpet displaying proudly all shades and mixtures of white, red, yellow and blue. The beautiful burnet rose and the bloody cranesbill are among the first summer flowers to show up. In July, the flower heads of ox-eye daisy (*Leucanthemum vulgare*) cover entire fields, and the shrubby cinquefoil (*Potentilla fruticosa*) paints the limestone around Mullagh More yellow. July and August are also the months when two of the Burren's most unmistakable and beautiful plants are in bloom: tutsan , a relative of St John's wort (*Hypercicum perforatum*), and the delicate yellow wort (*Blackstonia perfoliata*). Late summer provides a final treat in the form of the filigree white flowers of grass of Parnassus, while bell heather and ling/common heather form purple carpets.

Summer, it must be said, belongs to the orchids. Although the ancient belief that orchids were an aphrodisiac has long been disproved, these plants are still most enthralling. Orchids are strange. Their root system requires a special symbiosis with a fungus in order to produce flowers. Once the plant blooms – something that does not happen every year – the flowering period of each particular orchid species has to be timed to fit the life cycle of the pollinating insect species. From June onwards, the spotted orchids start to flower, among them O'Kelly's spotted orchid. They are followed by the mimicking fly orchid, lesser butterfly orchid and bee orchid in July. August is the time of pyramidal orchid, fragrant orchid (*Gymnadenia conopsea*) and the dark-red helleborine that grows mainly on the higher slopes of the limestone hills. The last – and one of the rarest orchids – is the autumn lady's tresses, which blooms in late August and flowers until late September. Probably the best places to encounter orchids are the Burren National Park and the Fanore dunes, whose grassy patches on the landward side are virtually covered with orchids.

Summer is also the time when the few day-active moths can be seen. Among the dozen diurnal – day-flying – species, the black-and-red-coloured burnets are the most eye-catching. Its body juices are poisonous, and its colours are a warning to predators. Larvae of butterflies also emerge at this time of the year; probably the most colourful is the orange-and-black-striped caterpillar of the cinnabar moth (*Tyria jacobaea*), which feeds entirely on ragwort (*Senecio jacobaea*). Sometimes six or more caterpillars can be found on one plant. Around the wetlands, several species of dragonfly are most active, and the meadows of the Burren are humming with the sounds of grasshoppers, bumblebees and other busy insects.

On a hot summer's day, it is not unusual to encounter Ireland's only native reptile: the common lizard (*Lacerta vivipara*) likes to sunbathe on the warm limestone rock, but disappears at the slightest hint of danger. Another species, the green lizard (*Lacerta viridis*), was released in the Burren in 1958, but apparently died out. In the late 1960s, the slow worm (*Anguis fragilis*) – a legless lizard – was also introduced to the Burren, and regular sightings – mainly in the north-eastern region – suggests it has established itself.

The light winds and calm sea of the summer months present the perfect opportunity to explore the Burren coastline. The Rine Peninsula, the Flaggy Shore at Finavarra and the limestone coast from Ballyryan to Black Head provide an insight into another

Lough Bunny (right), on the eastern border of the Burren, is the deepest lake in the Burren wetlands. The water level drops considerably in spring and summer, exposing parts of the limestone pavement that forms the bottom of the lake.

world. Mussels, barnacles and limpets cling to the rocks, and seaweed forests of many colours and forms sway slowly in the swell. In the rock pools of the intertidal zone, dog whelks (*Nucella lapillus*), sea urchins (*Echinus esculentus*) and common starfish (*Asterias rubens*) are looking for prey. Hermit crabs (*Eupagurus bernhardus*) and tiny prawns (*Leander serratus*) engage in their obscure activity. Occasionally, the strange-looking sea hare (*Aplysia punctata*) or a common jellyfish (*Aurelia aurita*) gets stuck in the pools, and must wait for the next high tide. Anglers line the coastline from Ballyryan to Ballyvaghan hoping for a catch of pollack (*Pollachius pollachius*) or wrasse (*Crenilabrus melops*).

In July and August, the Burren is packed with visitors. Countless bus loads stop here and there; there are the campers, cyclists, walkers and rock climbers – each one exploring and experiencing the Burren in a different way, and each one making an impact. Those visiting the Burren are wanted and welcome, and everybody should encounter this place at least once in their life, but every visitor is also a potential threat to its fragile ecosystem.

From mid-August, the landscape of the Burren begins to change. The transformation of bracken from dark green to a rich brown and the appearance of red berries on the hawthorn indicate that summer is at an end.

From early summer, the fields are being cut to prepare food
for cattle and sheep to bring them through the winter months.
Traditional hay-making (left) is in decline, as most farmers
have switched to the production of silage. Mown, sunburnt
fields (above) are emblematic of summer on a farm.

Bright summer days and blue skies make Leamaneh Castle appear less threatening. The remains of a house, deer park and walled garden (right) are visible east of the manor house.

In summer, the open limestone is transformed by an explosion of colour. The bloody cranesbill *(right)* is found in abundance all over the Burren. Tutsan *(below)* is another woodland plant that manages to survive on the open limestone inside the crevices. Hemp agrimony *(Eupatorium cannabinum)* *(below right)* is confined to the limestone pavement of the western quarter of the Burren.

The view from Corkscrew Hill is breathtaking. Ballyvaghan Valley is framed by Moneen and Aillwee Mountain to the right and Poulacapple and Cappanawalla to the left. Beyond lie the waters of Galway Bay, and even further are the mountains of Connemara.

The harebell (Campanula rotundifolia) *(right)* is a Burren glory found in abundance from the coast to the mountain summits. The unmistakable yellow wort *(above)* is a relative of the spring gentian. The strange thyme broomrape (Orobanche alba) *(above right)* is often mistaken for an orchid; a parasite, it obtains its nutrients from the plant to which it is attached – in this case, wild thyme.

Rathbourney Church is a late-medieval church located at the entrance of the valley lying between Cappanawalla and Poulacapple. It is thought to have been the primary church of the ruling O'Lochlain clan around the sixteenth century. The holy-water font (right) remains intact.

A magnificent Burren sunrise (above); from behind the Turloughmore Mountains in the eastern Burren the sun comes into view.

The mute swan (Cygnus olor) (far right) is common on the lakes of the Burren and around Ballyvaghan Bay. An especially large group seems to be resident on Lough Murree (above opposite) near Finavarra. The chicks (right) hatch in spring and stay with their parents well into the winter months.

Ancient stonewalls snake across the valleys and mountains (above) and abandoned farmhouses are common; this one (right) overlooks Caher Valley.

The summer belongs to the butterflies and moths.
The small tortoiseshell (above) and the common
blue (right) are among the more common species.

Ballyvaghan Valley from the slopes of Aillwee Mountain.

Summer in the Burren is synonymous with orchids. The rare fly orchid (above) is found mainly in the southeast of the Burren. The lesser butterfly orchid (right) and the pyramidal orchid (above right) are more abundant.

*O'Kelly's spotted orchid (above left) is a Burren speciality; the pure-
white form of the common spotted orchid, it was discovered by
Bernard O'Kelly, a Burren farmer. The flecked marsh orchid (above
right), another rare species, is restricted to the turloughs and lakes
of the south-eastern Burren. A typical flower of the open limestone
and another Burren speciality is the dark-red helleborine (right).*

This hawthorn bush grows at the foot of the cliffs of Kinallia. Lone hawthorn bushes are said to be the home of fairies, and interfering with them brings harm or even death.

Early-morning light is cast towards the foot of Slieve Carran (above). The early hours of a Burren summer sunrise are often quite magical. The 'green road' winding along the northern slope of Abbey Hill offers a breathtaking view of Galway Bay; the roadside is adorned with flowers and bracken (right).

The Caher River tumbles down the Khyber Pass en route to the Atlantic Ocean at Fanore (right). Deserted farmsteads – such as this at Caher Valley – provide a glimpse of how life once was. In the shelter of the valley, trees can grow to an impressive height (below).

The Caher River has its source deep inside the Caher Valley, which lies between Slieve Elva and Poulacapple (above). The Caher Valley Nature Reserve – founded by the late John MacNamara – occupies a small part of the valley. In August, the nuts of the hazel appear; still green, they are a first hint of summer's end (left).

During hot summer days the beach at Fanore and the adjoining dune system are a favourite recreation place for locals and visitors alike. In the evening, silence once again descends.

Ballyvaghan Bay on a calm summer morning; in the distance, the slopes of Gleninagh Mountain descend towards the sea (above). The common limpet (Patella vulgaris) *is just one of countless shellfish and fish species that populate the Burren shores (right).*

Kinvarra in County Galway marks the north-eastern border of the Burren. Once the most important harbour in the area, it links Connemara with the Burren (above). Crushed shells and limestone pepper the shorelines along the north-eastern coast of the Burren (right).

Late summer produces a new reign of colour: wild thyme (Thymus praecox) (above left) – the wild form of garden thyme – can be used for cooking. Shrubby cinquefoil (above) – a Burren speciality – is confined to the shores of the lakes and turloughs of the eastern Burren, and will become submerged when the water level rises later in the year. The grass of Parnassus – one of the most delicate flowers in the Burren – (left) blooms from late August.

Devil's-bit scabious (Succisa pratensis) (above left), another flower to bloom in late summer, is common throughout the Burren. Water mint (above right) grows in damp places – even in water – and can produce flowers until October. Bell heather (opposite left) and ling/common heather (opposite right) – both common across the Burren – are a sure sign of the coming autumn.

In the northern Burren the waters around Aughinish Island (above) and at the Rine Peninsula (left) are almost motionless under the summer skies.

Kinturley tidal mill, near Aughinish Bay – established in 1804 – operated well into the twentieth century. Whether the building will withstand the power of the tides is an open question.

A thunderstorm shrouds the Burren uplands at Slieve Elva. Commercial forestation has been a feature of this area since 1960; most of the planted trees are non-native Sitka spruce (Picea sitchensis).

A shower rains down on Turlough Hill; the increased frequency of rain forecasts the approach of autumn.

A last summer sunset on the limestone pavement on the Burren's west coast. Out in the Atlantic, the storms of autumn are brewing.

CHAPTER FOUR

AUTUMN

*The rising sun peaks through the clouds; its warm
rays bathe the stony Burren coast at Ballyryan.*

THERE are still some warm and sunny days in September, but the nights are cold and the hours of daylight are in noticeable decline. Heavy rain and gale-force winds once again buffet the Burren coast. Yet autumn is a colourful time when the shrubs and trees of the Burren proudly display their foliage and fruit. The nuts of hazel are ripe, the juicy and tasty fruits of bramble (*Rubus fruticosus*) can be found almost everywhere, and blackthorn is laden with succulent blue-black sloes. Bearberry (*Arctostaphylos uva-ursi*) offers small orange-red berries, the attractive red berries of the guelder rose come in clusters, and the pink fruits of the spindle (*Euonymus europaeus*) and the red berries of holly (*Ilex aquifolium*) are plentiful.

Shrubs and trees are an important element within Irish folklore. Foremost among them is the hawthorn, whose deep-red berries are emblematic of autumn. As the home or meeting place of the fairies, interfering with these fairy thorns will bring bad luck. Hazel, blackthorn and ash (*Fraxinus excelsior*) are thought to protect against evil, whereas elder (*Sambucus nigra*) – found mainly in hedgerows – is said to be an unlucky tree.

The ash stands as the master tree in the few Burren woodlands or as a single, often windswept, individual on the open limestone. In autumn, the ash is a beautiful sight: the bright bark gleams in the sunshine and the characteristic deep-brown fruits – the ash keys – remain attached to the branches long after the leaves have fallen.

Some flowers also produce fruit. The hips of the burnet rose change their colour from burgundy-red to dark-blue, and the berry-like fruits of tutsan are transformed from bright green, through red to dark blue.

This abundance of food is of enormous benefit to the animals of the Burren; pine marten and badger are partial to a meal of blackberries, squirrels fatten on a diet of hazelnuts, and birds feast on the fruits of the guelder rose or the bright-red berries of lords and ladies – berries that are poisonous for most mammals.

The appearance of the Burren changes completely during the months of autumn. In early September, the blues and purples of knapweed (*Centaurea scabiosa*), devil's-bit scabious and harebell are evidence of a valiant effort to prolong summer, but finally – like all the other Burren flowers – they fade away. Some flowers make one last showing: the burnet rose paints its leaves orange red, the leaves of tutsan shimmer in all the colours of the rainbow, and the mountain avens produces beautiful feather-like seed heads.

By the end of September, the foliage of shrubs and trees has changed from the green of summer to bright yellow and red tones. After turning brown, the dry and crisp leaves fall to the ground, leaving behind naked, skeleton-like trunks and branches. The grasses are also losing their summer gown, and the once-green fields now present several shades of brown.

A misty morning at Muckinish Bay (right) in the evening, while skies of blue provide the backdrop to Abbey Hill (far right).

Although most plants are preparing for their well-deserved winter break, some are only now commencing their activities. The ubiquitous ivy (*Hedera helix*) starts to bloom in October, producing shoots crowned with green panicles that will turn into black berries by spring and provide a favourite food for blackbirds (*Turdus merula*). Mushrooms and toadstools – the reproductive parts of underground living fungi – make their short appearance above ground; shaggy ink cap (*Coprinus comatus*) and milk cap (*Lactarius torminosus*), parasol (*Lepiota procera*), honey fungus (*Armillaria mellea*) and others turn up in the grassy patches and woodlands of the Burren.

Autumn is an outstanding season for observing seabirds. Kittiwakes (*Rissa tridactyla*), fulmars (*Fulmarus glacialis*), gannets (*Morus bassanus*) and others leave their breeding grounds along Irish and British coasts to spend winter on the open Atlantic; during September and October, line after line pass the limestone coast at Black Head during their annual migration. Once the summer visitors have gone, the winter residents return from their Arctic breeding grounds. By the end of October, the first arrivals – brent geese, white-fronted geese (*Anser albifrons*) and whooper swan (*Cygnus cygnus*) – have settled at Galway Bay and the turloughs.

From the Burren coast, seals are a regular sight. The common seal (*Phoca vitulina*) breeds on Tawin Island and Illaunloo on the inshore parts of Galway Bay, while grey seals (*Halichoerus grypus*) come down from Connemara to feed. Common dolphins (*Dephinus delphis*) and harbour porpoises (*Phocoena phocoena*) can be encountered regularly as they follow the fish that feed on the abundant plankton of Galway Bay. Sightings of whales are rare but possible; minke whales (*Balaenoptera acutorostrata*) and pilot whales (*Globicephala melas*) follow the coastline on their mysterious migration routes.

As the tourist season comes to an end in late September, the farmers of the Burren bring their animals to higher grounds, where they will spend the winter. This ancient practice is based on the knowledge that the limestone hills of the Burren, like a giant storage heater, build up heat in summer and dissipate it in winter when the surrounding climate is cooler, thus prolonging growth of the Burren vegetation; only occasionally will cattle and sheep need to be provided with additional food. Winterage is also an important conservation practice, as the animals' consumption of old grasses ensures that the delicate Burren flowers will thrive next year.

Autumn can be a short season, lasting only a few weeks. By the end of October, trees and shrubs have lost their foliage, most of the berries are gone, and the sleepy mood of winter has descended upon the Burren.

The aptly named autumn gentian (Gentianella amarelle) *(opposite left)* is one of the last flowers to bloom. *The flowers of the common spotted orchid (opposite right) are slowly fading away. The mountain avens (above) shows its seed heads.*

By mid-September, the shrubby cinquefoil (top left) has withered, while tutsan (top right) displays its berry-like fruits. The seeds of the hemp agrimony (opposite left) are soon blown away by the brisk autumn winds. The ash – the Burren's most common tree – (opposite right) is swiftly losing its leaves, but keeps its winged seeds.

Carron church, located in the very heart of the Burren, is a typical medieval parish church. The church is thought to have had an upper storey that would have been used as living quarters for the priest.

The Cistercian abbey at Corcomroe, Sancta Maria de Petra Fertili (St Mary of the Fertile Rock), is situated at the foot of Abbey Hill and is the most impressive building of its kind in the Burren. Founded in the thirteenth century by the O'Brien family, it houses the tomb of King Conor O'Brien, who died in battle in 1268. 'His body was honourably interred in the monastery of East Burren by the monks of that convent who also raised a grand marble figure to his memory.' (Wars of Turlough Chronicles).

The gatehouse of the abbey – located around 100 metres west of the church – is one of the few outbuildings still standing.

*The view from a window of the
south chapel of Corcomroe Abbey.*

By October, Lough Gealáin (right), at the foot of Mullagh More, has reclaimed most of the land it had conceded during spring and summer. A calm and clear autumn day allows a perfect reflection of Knockanes mountain on the surface of Lough Gealáin (above).

Hawthorn at the foot of Moneen Mountain (above) and on the lower slopes of Gleninagh Mountain (left). The bushes have lost their leaves but the bright-red berries can remain on the shrubs well into winter.

Dunguaire Castle (above), built in the sixteenth century on a small peninsula at Kinvarra Bay, is probably the best-preserved tower house in the Burren. It was purchased by Lady Christabel Ampthill in 1954; following restoration, the castle was opened to the public in 1966. Shanmuckinish Castle (left) – the 'old castle at Muckinish' – was witness to the execution in 1584 of O'Loughlin, who was captured here by O'Brien and executed following his trial in Ennis.

Late-autumn fog can persist all day, giving the Burren an eerie aspect.

*Autumn is berry time; the blackthorn (right) and hawthorn (above)
produce berries equal in beauty to their flowers. The blue-black fruits
of blackthorn are traditionally used in the production of sloe gin.
The primary location of the scarce alder buckthorn (Frangula alnus)
(above right) is close to a number of turloughs in the eastern Burren.*

The fruits of the guelder rose *(left) are extremely poisonous when consumed by man yet harmless to birds. The snowberry (Symphoricarpos albus) (above) – a garden shrub that escaped into the wild – is now widespread in the Burren.*

*Ballyvaghan Valley where the greens of
summer have given way to autumn browns.*

The holy well at MacDuagh's hermitage is said to cure backache. A nearby blackthorn is adorned with relics deposited by summer pilgrims.

The mountains of Turloughmore, Knockanes and Mullagh More (above) form a backdrop to the limestone pavement of Keelhilla. Leaves of hazel (far left) and burnet rose (left) add a dash of colour to a gloomy autumn scene.

The juicy berries of the bramble (above) and the nuts of the hazel (top right) are a prized Burren crop. The fruits of the stone bramble (Rubus saxatilis) (right) are also edible, though not as tasty as those of its cousin.

*The fruits – or hips – of the burnet rose (above right) ripen from
a bright-red to black. The spindle tree (Euonymus europaeus)
(top) produces the most delicate fruit. The poisonous holly
(above left) is still widely used as a Christmas decoration.*

Lough Bunny (above) has risen considerably and the summer shoreline is again submerged. In the distance on the opposite shore stands the ruin of a tower house. A typical autumn morning: threatening clouds endeavour to obscure the sun (left).

Dromore Lake and Dromore Castle are situated in the midst of the Dromore Wood National Nature Reserve at the south-eastern border of the Burren. Each year, a pair of ravens nest on the castle; after breeding, the ravens depart, to be replaced by a pair of kestrels.

Bishopsquarter: storm clouds approaching Ballyvaghan Bay from the west occur regularly at this time of the year.

The availability of food along the coast of the Burren encourages numerous birds to settle here. The rook (Corvus frugilegus) (above) and herring gull (Larus argentatus) (left) are resident species.

The redshank (Tringa totanus) (above) is typically a winter visitor, though some individuals stay all year round. The whooper swan arrives from its breeding grounds in Iceland (right) in October and stays until March.

As the days shorten, the magical light of an autumn sun illuminates the limestone pavement of the western Burren from Ballyryan to Black Head.

A sky of pastel colours and low-hanging clouds (above). A beam of light finds its way into the valleys of the Burren (left).

A subterranean connection with the sea accounts for the brackish appearance of Lough Murree, thought to be one of the most nutrient-rich waters of the Burren. The resident mute swans are joined by many winter visitors such as pochard (Aythya ferina), *tufted duck* (Aythya fuligula) *and wigeon.*

Late-autumn leaves form a carpet in the Caher Valley Nature Reserve (above). The Caher River, almost dry in summer, is once again replenished (left).

The damp but mild climate of autumn brings out many species of fungi. The delicate porcelain fungus (Oudemansiella mucida) (opposite top) and the unmistakable orange peel (Peziza aurantia) (opposite left) prefer woodlands, whereas the agarics (gill fungi) (opposite right) are content with a cowpat.

The 'green road' at Abbey Hill is now in shadow most of the day (above). The flowers have disappeared from the roadside and the bracken has turned brown. The grass fades in colour alongside grey limestone walls (left).

A cold and breezy morning in late autumn plays host to a beautiful sunrise over Aughinish Bay.

CHAPTER FIVE

WINTER

*Eagle's Rock: a rare winter snowfall has coated
the cliffs of Kinallia and the plain of Keelhilla.*

WINTER in the Burren: six hours of daylight, endless rain, fog lingering in the valleys and storm clouds rushing in from the Atlantic. The wet limestone appears almost black, and the surrounding browns and yellows are only occasionally relieved by the evergreens of holly, ivy and yew (*Taxus baccata*). But winter in the Burren also brings crisp, fresh air, blue skies and warm sunshine.

The increased rainfall causes an expansion of the turloughs. The turlough at Carron is the biggest of its kind, flooding about 150 hectares (370 acres). Meadows, stone walls, trees and whole hedgerows disappear under water. Another fine example of a seasonal lake can be seen at the foot of Mullagh More; Lough Gealáin in summer is a small lake, but can more than treble in size in winter.

From October, the wetlands and sheltered coastal areas of the Burren attract an array of winter guests. Thousands of wading birds and wildfowl gather on the turloughs, lakes and around Galway Bay to feed. Curlew, lapwing, Greenland white-fronted goose (*Anser albifrons*), brent goose (*Branta bernicla*), whooper swan, wigeon and teal are just a few of the many species now in residence. The sheltered mudflat at the Rine Peninsula plays host to huge flocks of birds, and the coming and going of ducks and geese rouses the interest of birds of prey such as the peregrine and hen harrier; these magnificent birds usually hunt in the open meadows and hedgerows of the Burren, but the concentration of prey now draws them to the coast.

Winter offers an opportunity to glimpse the reclusive pine marten and its relative, the Irish stoat. The lack of foliage makes it much easier to observe these beautiful predators, and the reduction of daylight hours increases the chances of seeing them during the day.

Although heavy storms – often accompanied by lightning and hailstone – sweep over the Burren during the winter months, it

Snow is a rare event in the Burren; even when it does occur, it lasts no more than a day or two.

stays mild; frost is unusual and snow a rarity. These mild Burren winters are a product of the Atlantic Ocean and the open limestone releasing heat stored during the summer. Consequently, the growing period in the Burren is interrupted for only a short time, if at all, and it is no surprise to find primrose in bloom in November or herb Robert (*Geranium robertianum*) flowering at Christmas.

Winter is the season of ferns, mosses and lichens. Though present all year long, the leaves and grasses that usually obscure them have gone into decline, thus enabling them to receive the attention they deserve.

The bare branches of many shrubs and trees are covered with several species of lichen – a fungus involved in a symbiotic relationship with algae whereby the lichen is nourished by algae while the fungus covers and protects the algae from desiccation. Lichen is a living bio-monitoring device; its absorption of water and gases directly from the air makes it more sensitive to atmospheric pollution than other plants. In areas of high pollution, lichen gradually disappears.

Mosses need a damp environment to survive, and are found primarily in the crevices of the limestone or in the thick hazel shrubs; they are also abundant near the lakes and turloughs.

Fern – widespread in the Burren – is one of the oldest surviving plants; fossils have been dated to as long ago as 400 million years. Around 25 species of fern have been recorded in the Burren, among them the normally lime-shunning bracken – one of the most recognisable and widespread species here. Bracken is also one of the few species to die away in winter; from its dark green of summer, and yellow and bright shades of brown in autumn, it turns dark brown and – finally – virtually black in winter. Other easy-to-recognise species are Hart's tongue fern (*Phyllitis scolopendrium*) – the only fern with undivided leaves – and the sea spleenwort (*Asplenium marinum*), a coastal plant that only grows close to the ocean and likes to be splashed with sea water. The most beautiful ferns are the small species often hidden in crevices or fighting their way through layers of brown hazel leaves, among them the maidenhair spleenwort (*Asplenium trichomanes*) and rusty back fern (*Ceterach officinarum*), both common in the Burren, as is the unmistakable wall rue (*Asplenium ruta-muraria*). The occasional but far-from-rare maidenhair fern (*Adiantum capillusveneris*) is a Burren speciality; it usually grows in tropical and subtropical

regions, but in the Burren it can be found within a few centimetres of Arctic plant species.

In January, as winter seems to tighten its grip, the first flower of the year bursts into bloom: the winter heliotrope (*Petasites fragrans*) is no native plant but an escapee from gardens. Nevertheless, its delicate flowers are a welcome sight on a cold and wet day in January, and raise hopes of a better time to come.

The beach at Fanore is one of the gems of the Burren.
The limestone pavement, coloured by encrusting lichen, is
surrounded by golden sand. The adjoining dunes are
dominated by marram grass (Ammophila arenaria).

While winter storms batter the limestone coast (above), boats are kept safe in places like Ballyvaghan (right).

The relatively calm waters of Galway Bay provide winter shelter for numerous birds. Resident species mingle with visitors such as the common gull (Larus canus) (right), the brent goose and the pochard (above).

Winter storms deposit a variety of seaweeds on the upper shore; the drying process produces a vivid array of reds, browns and yellows. The common mussel (Mytilus edulis) *(right)* is an important source of food for many birds; cracked shells litter the shore.

The flowers of the Burren are capable of a special beauty in winter; witness the withering seed heads of yellow wort (above top) and tufted vetch (Vicia cracca) (right), or the remnants of the flowers of greater knapweed (above).

The birds have overlooked the last berry of this guelder rose (above left). The dried fruits of tutsan (above right) and the seed heads of goldenrod (far left) disappear during the winter months, but the faded carline thistle (Carlina vulgaris) (left) can remain until the following spring.

Carron Turlough: after Galway Bay, it is the most important wintering site for birds. When fully flooded, it is around 3 kilometres long and half a kilometre wide, and covers more than 150 hectares.

The seasonal lake at Turlough (below far left) has appeared almost overnight, submerging fields, walls and hedgerows. Lough Bunny (left top) has reached its highest level by December. The limestone hills in the distance are usually shrouded by mist or cloud.

Mullagh More (left) and its neighbour Knockanes (right) are at their most majestic in winter. Lough Gealáin – having more than doubled in size – has swallowed the limestone pavement and its shrubs.

The tree at this old Caher Valley farmstead (left) has long since lost its foliage. These old farmhouses are often used as shelter for animals during winter. The heavy rains have made the 'green road' ascending Slieve Elva impassable (above).

Cairns and portal tombs – ancient burial sites – are among the oldest buildings in the Burren. The beginnings of Poulawack cairn (above) date back to around 3350 BC; the place was used and extended for more than 2,000 years. Wedge tombs such as this at Parknabinnia (left) are numerous in the Burren; they were built between 2300-2000 BC.

These skeletons of hazel (below left) and ash (below right) accentuate the sense of loneliness at remote Keelhilla, the place chosen by St Colman MacDuagh for his hermitage.

A lone hawthorn at the cliffs of Kinallia (right). The hazel wood (below) that surrounds St Colman MacDuagh's church is thought to be one of the oldest in the Burren.

Cattle (right) are kept outside during the winter;
like the feral goat, cattle remove dead grasses like
in Ballyryan (above) and cut back shrubs, thus
enabling flowers and herbs to grow again in spring.

The feral goats have grown thick winter coats (above) and can be seen roaming the steep limestone cliffs in search of edible parts of shrubs (left).

Though fern species such as Hart's tongue fern (opposite top right) and bracken (opposite bottom right) wither away in winter, others are at their best during this cold and wet season. Sea spleenwort (above) is typical in crevices near the coast. Maidenhair spleenwort (opposite bottom left) and rusty back fern (opposite top left) are probably the most beautiful and abundant ferns of the Burren.

The Rine Peninsula and its adjoining saltmarsh, located on the western side of Ballyvaghan Bay, is one of the most beautiful and environmentally important places of the Burren; home to most of the wintering waders and wildfowl – including up to a hundred brent geese – it also provides a habitat for the rare otter (Lutra lutra).

*The boulders on the limestone pavement at Black Head were
deposited by retreating glaciers around 10,000 years ago
(opposite left). The limestone fields in the eastern Burren
following a blizzard in late December: the clouds threaten yet
more snow and sleet (above left). Remnants of last summer's
grass wither in the crevices of the limestone (above right).*

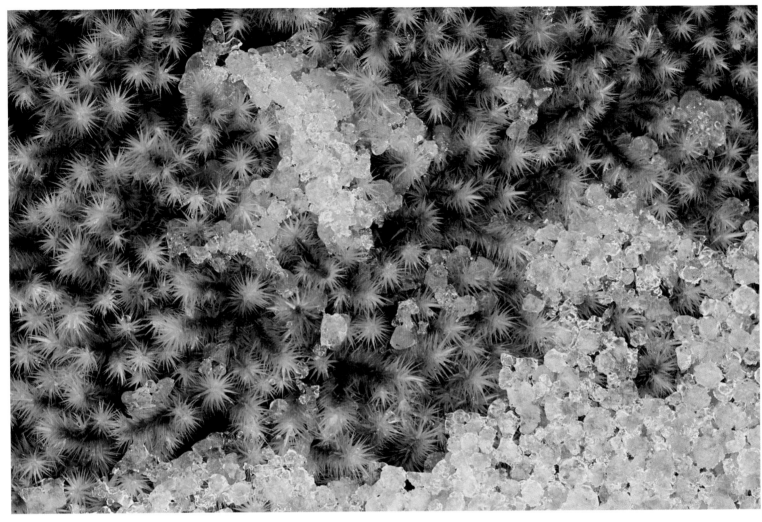

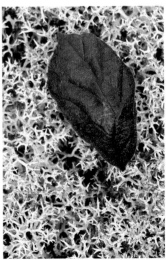

Mosses (opposite top and bottom far left), liverworts (opposite bottom middle) and lichens (opposite bottom right and above) – abundant in the Burren – are concealed by grass and foliage for most of the year; winter reveals their presence.

Templecronan – a small oratory near Carron – is thought to have been built in the twelfth century; several carved heads of men and animals decorate its walls.

Kilfenora and its cathedral (left) are located at the southern tip of the Burren. The village first rose to importance when it became the seat of the bishop in 1152. Today, it is a major centre for tourism and houses the Burren Visitor Centre, the first of its kind. Kilfenora's group of high crosses date from the twelfth century; the west cross (above) – located in a field 200 metres west of the cathedral – stands more than 4.5 metres high.

The rapid change from sunny spells to heavy showers brings extra colour to a Burren winter, the season of rainbows.

Mild temperatures ensure plant life never really comes to a total stop; mountain avens (below left) maintain green leaves even in January, and the ground covering of moss and ivy takes advantage of the damp conditions (above left).

January sees the first signs of spring: hazel catkins (opposite left) and buds (opposite top right) spring to life. The very first flower of the year, the winter heliotrope (opposite bottom right) – a garden escapee – bursts into bloom in late January.

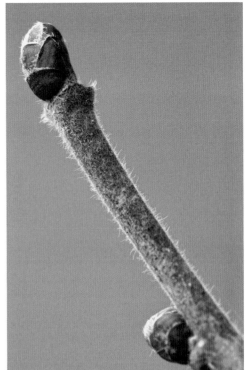

The winter sun casts a spell of golden light over Caher Valley (above). At the Caher Valley Nature Reserve, the Caher River carries more water than ever (right).

*Late January in Bishopsquarter
provides the first hints of spring.*

THE BURREN CODE

The people of the Burren welcome visitors to Ireland's most extraordinary landscape. The Burren may look rugged, but it is a fragile place and is under threat from increased human activity. The people who live in the Burren depend on the landscape for their livelihoods in agriculture and tourism. The limestone pavement, flora and built heritage are the resources upon which tourism in the Burren thrives. Respecting and conserving this resource will sustain the community's well-being. Please respect the Burren Code and help protect the limestone pavement, plants and built heritage of this irreplaceable 'fertile rock'.

· Much of the limestone pavement is private property and is being farmed in the traditional way so as to maintain the limestone landscape. Avoid damaging walls and pavement, and respect the privacy of landowners.
· Please desist from building miniature cairns and dolmens; these damage the shattered limestone pavements and compromise the natural landscape.
· Never remove weathered limestone from the Burren, and avoid buying souvenirs or products made of weathered limestone. It is illegal to remove stone from the pavement or boundary walls. Limestone pavement is protected under the European Habitats Directive (92/43/EEC).
· More than 700 different flowering plants and ferns have been recorded in the Burren; though the Burren represents only 1 per cent of the landmass of Ireland, 75 per cent of Irish native species are contained in the area. Help protect the wildflowers of the Burren: never pick flowers or remove plants or tamper with their habitats. It is prohibited to pick or uproot plants in national parks and nature reserves. Parking on the limestone pavement or grassland damages habitats.
· The built heritage of the Burren has evolved over the past 5,000 years. Sites such as prehistoric tombs, monasteries and ringforts are well known, but traditional houses, field walls and ancient road systems are also vital to the unique character of the Burren. Take care not to disturb any of these monuments, and respect all of the built heritage. It is illegal to deface, damage or remove any part of the built heritage.

The Burren Code was devised by the Burren Tourism Joint Steering Committee, comprising representatives of Clare County Council, Dúchas (the Heritage Service) and Shannon Development in partnership with the tourism industry, local-community groups and environmental-interest groups.

A POSSIBLE FUTURE

The year is 2036. The Burren has changed. Farming is a thing of the past. The last Burren farmer had to quit and give up his farm in 2026. Cheap milk and meat imports from abroad and the invention of artificial milk in 2016 forced not only the Burren farmers but also all farmers in the west of Ireland to give up their livelihood and look for work in other areas. Luckily, a huge increase in visitors triggered by major developments in the tourism sector saved the area from an economic disaster.

The farms and dwellings in the Burren uplands are almost all abandoned. Settlement now concentrates along the coast where modern housing developments serve the remaining local residents and the countless visitors. The outskirts of traditional tourist villages like Ballyvaghan and Doolin have grown into huge holiday home and entertainment parks that are overlooked by some of the biggest hotel complexes ever built in Ireland. The Fanore golf and tennis club opened in 2020 and has grown into the most frequented facility of its kind in County Clare.

However, this tourist boom seems to be coming to an end. Visitor numbers are dropping. The most likely reason for this development is that the astonishing Burren landscape is almost gone. The once green meadows and the grey limestone pavements and summits are overgrown by hazel and hawthorn thickets. Most of the flowering plants, including the spring gentian and most orchid species, have been declared extinct. Also gone is the Irish hare. Sightings of the pine marten happen occasionally but the animal seems to have retreated into the most remote and inaccessible hazel woods. The slaughter of the Burren feral goats that started in the early years of the millennia ended in 2010 when the last of the goats was shot dead. The loss of all grazing animals – wild and domestic – and a constantly warming and more humid climate resulted in the explosion of hazel and hawthorn and the retreat and extinction of almost all other plants.

To save at least parts of the unique Burren heritage the long debated visitor centre at Mullagh More has been built and recently opened its gates for visitors. The Mullagh More Experience and Conservation Park is state of the art in information and entertainment. Three huge glass domes host the last original species of the famous Burren flora in a recreated Burren landscape based on reports and pictures of the late twentieth century. The Poulnabrone portal tomb and other selected heritage sites have been relocated into one of the domes to be preserved for the future.

If this project is successful other similar conservation parks are planned for the former nature reserve at Keelhila in the heart of the Burren and for the stretch of coast between the outskirts of Doolin town and Ballyryan village.

There is hope that these projects will save at least parts of the unique Burren heritage for future generations …

AFTERWORD

Whatever the future may hold for the Burren, if we may or may not change our behaviour and remember that we are a part of our earth not its master, I would like to close this book like it started with some lines from Luka Bloom …

I walk with my father in Fanore
We walk hand in hand by the shore
The sun sets beyond Inisheer
I thank you for bringing me here.

Where the limestone slopes down to the sea
Where my father walks tall, proud and free
Where the birdsong is music to my ear
I thank you for bringing me here.

Luka Bloom
www.lukabloom.com

(© by Luka Bloom, lyrics reproduced with kind permission, 'Thank you for bringing me here' taken from the Luka Bloom album *Innocence*)

Thank you for bringing me there …

EQUIPMENT

For photographing the images in this book, I used digital SLR cameras, with lenses from 18mm to 500mm, including a 105mm and a 180mm macro lens. The panorama images were shot with a Hasselblad XPAN camera with a 45mm lens on Fuji Velvia 50 transparency film. Besides the cameras, the most important tool was a tripod with removable centre column – to get as close to the ground as possible – and a pan/tilt head or a ball head depending on what I was shooting.

Filters were also essential. I used the Cokin P system with a polarizer, several graduated grey filters, some warm-ups and a grey filter. To produce evenly exposed panorama transparencies, a centre-spot filter was used with the Hasselblad XPAN camera.

Other equipment included a waist-level finder attached to the camera hot-shoe, cable releases, gold/silver reflectors, diffusers and a plant clamp to steady long-stemmed flowers.

BIBLIOGRAPHY

Cunningham, George, *Burren Journey*, Shannonside Mid-Western Regional Tourism Organisation, 1978.

Cunningham, George, *Burren Journey North*, Burren Research Press, 1992.

Cunningham, George, *Burren Journey West*, Shannonside Mid-western Regional Tourism Organisation, 1980.

Cunningham, George, *Exploring the Burren*, Town House and Country House, 1998.

D'Arcy, Gordon, *A Natural History of the Burren*, Immel Publishing, 1992.

Dunford, Brendan, *Farming and the Burren*, Teagasc, 2002.

Feehan, John M., *The Secret Places of the Burren*, Royal Carbery Books, 1987.

Jones, Carlton, *The Burren and the Aran Islands – Exploring the Archaeology*, The Collins Press, 2004.

Mac Coitir, Niall, *Irish Trees – Myths, Legends and Folklore*, The Collins Press, 2003.

Mitchell, Frank and Ryan, Michael, *Reading the Irish Landscape*, Town House and Country House, 1986.

Nelson, Charles, *The Burren – A Companion to the Wildflowers of an Irish Limestone Wilderness*, Conservancy of the Burren Ltd./Samton Ltd., 1997.

Nelson, Charles, *Wild Plants of the Burren and the Aran Islands*, The Collins Press, 1999.

Poyntz, Sarah, *A Burren Journal*, Tír Eolas, 2000.

Robinson, Tim, *The Burren Map*, Folding Landscapes, 1999.

Sterry, Paul, *Complete British Wildlife Photoguide*, Harper Collins, 1997.

Sterry, Paul, *Complete Irish Wildlife Photoguide*, Harper Collins, 2004.